FIFTY-FOUR
Sylmar Branch Library
14561 Polk Street
Sylmar, CA 91342

P9-CQS-084

This Book Comes With Lots of FREE Online Resources

Nolo's award-winning website has a page dedicated just to this book. Here you can:

KEEP UP TO DATE. When there are important changes to the information in this book, we'll post updates.

GET DISCOUNTS ON NOLO PRODUCTS. Get discounts on hundreds of books, forms, and software.

READ BLOGS. Get the latest info from Nolo authors' blogs.

LISTEN TO PODCASTS. Listen to authors discuss timely issues on topics that interest you.

WATCH VIDEOS. Get a quick introduction to a legal topic with our short videos.

And that's not all.
Nolo.com contains thousands of articles on everyday legal and business issues, plus a plain-English law dictionary, all written by Nolo experts and available for free. You'll also find more useful **books, software, online apps, downloadable forms,** plus a **lawyer directory.**

With **Downloadable FORMS**

NOLO
LAW for ALL

Get forms and more at
www.nolo.com/back-of-book/NON.html

NOLO

The Trusted Name

(but don't take our word for it)

"In Nolo you can trust."

THE NEW YORK TIMES

"Nolo is always there in a jam as the nation's premier publisher of do-it-yourself legal books."

NEWSWEEK

"Nolo publications... guide people simply through the how, when, where and why of the law."

THE WASHINGTON POST

"[Nolo's]... material is developed by experienced attorneys who have a knack for making complicated material accessible."

LIBRARY JOURNAL

"When it comes to self-help legal stuff, nobody does a better job than Nolo..."

USA TODAY

"The most prominent U.S. publisher of self-help legal aids."

TIME MAGAZINE

"Nolo is a pioneer in both consumer and business self-help books and software."

LOS ANGELES TIMES